GET FRESH BOOKS

Praise for *Dear Inheritors*

Dear Inheritors is written for you—regardless of your politics, race, or class. At once tender and brutally honest, Kathy Engel's poetic letter to her readers reveals the everyday "hurricane" that lives "under the belly of the good life"—unnamed inequities, the "tattoo of two worlds divided by train tracks," witness masquerading as activism. But the same poems that indict, also console, encourage us. Yes, we "live inside contradictions," still we are learning "who can we keep alive" and what a "do-over" might look like. Part metaphor, part instructions for repair, Engel's collection taunts us, lyrics us—ultimately, heals us.

> **—Kimberly Blaeser,** author of *Ancient Light*, past Wisconsin
> Poet Laureate

Kathy Engel stands open, vulnerable, in a vast world "Where the mirror is confused[.]" and does not flinch. She refuses her own world's "thousand masks" of denial, even when anguish or privilege tempt or obfuscate. Her lyricism and her direct speech live among tables, blessing bowls, and gardens; horses, wild birds, and public art; "spit, paste, memory, hammer;" and always the sea, her beloved Atlantic where the waters live and where she physically tunes her attention to far songs. Engel wears a mantle of poet-citizen lightly but authentically, bearing a decades-rich devotion to and work inside literary and social justice communities. Who dares to sing of "we" or "us" while inhabiting a place "where land stays stolen/swollen?" This book declares "we are more than the names/of places, more than lists—" and it lives there/here at soul-level. Engel's clarity and conscience also embrace a tender mortality— "even when the severing is slow[.]" *Dear Inheritors* addresses populi.

> **-Judith Vollmer** is the author of six books of poetry, including
> most recently *The Sound Boat: New & Selected Poems*
> (University of Wisconsin 2022).

Audre Lorde once asked "where is true history written, except in the poems?" In Dear Inheritors we experience the interconnected love-scale of a being committed to beauty in the form of freedom for all oppressed people, accountability in the form of interspecies presence, and grace in the form of ongoing witness, whether witnessing a mimosa tree in the yard, a loved one, the ebbs and flows of a movement or the porous self, transformed by all of it. This book will help you remember how to be *here*, lovingly, curiously inside whichever indescribable moment you face.

> **—Alexis Pauline Gumbs,** PhD, is the author of six books including most recently *Survival Is a Promise: The Eternal Life of Audre Lorde* (Macmillan 2024).

Get Fresh Publishing, A Non-Profit Corp.
PO Box 901
Union, NJ 07083

www.gfbpublishing.org

ISBN: 9798218404475

Library of Congress Control Number: 2024935734
Cover, layout, typesetting, and design:
Anny Caba | AnnyCaba.com

Cover Art: "Learning Library Landings" by Darlene Charnecort.

This book was typeset in Futura Std, Helvetica, and Times New Roman

CONTENTS

DEAR
INHERITORS

BY KATHY ENGEL

for my sisters Susan & Jenno

for my sister Alexis

& for the people of Gaza

*... Like you I
love love, life, the sweet smell
of things....*
–Roque Dalton, "Like You"
Translated by Jack Hirschman

*...Will you ever bring a better gift for the world
than the breathing respect that you carry
wherever you go right now?*
–William Stafford, "You Reading This, Be Ready"

...We have poetry so we will not die of history...
–Meena Alexander, "Question Time"

Preface

The South African poet Keorapetse Kgositsile once wrote about how the present
was a dangerous place to live. One reads the poetry of Kathy Engel and one is
unfortunately reminded that this continues to be true. *DEAR INHERITORS*
is a collection that seems to be an open letter to the world. What is the
difference between inheritors and survivors? What if writing letters today
has become a lost art? Where are our envelopes and stamps?

Engel in this book defines herself as a white Jewish American woman.
She writes while navigating issues of race as well as the realities of Gaza.
Engel celebrates the body in much the same manner Walt Whitman
did while embracing the earth.

When I was a new green spear
of grass I reached up fast as
I could, knowing the air is
ours, hoping to evade
the blade, motors whose handlers
regard me as something to control

The long lines of Whitman can be found in Engel's "Where I Live."
The poem is a poetic memoir of coming of age and helps to open the door
to a collection that shares with us Japanese forms of haiku, tanka
and haibun.

Engel writes poetry that surprises the living and the living room.
Her work slow dances with the voice of June Jordan. There are horses
running free in this book and one thinks of Joy Harjo and this too
connects Engel to the exploration of death. How can one ignore how
the poem "Unmarked Graves of Indigenous Children, 2021" finds its
companion with "What's Another Word for Genocide?"

At times it seems we expect too much from our poets. Yet without them
how can a people see or have faith in the future? What is there to
inherit if we reduce the world to ruins? Gaza was once a place but
now language has turned it into a metaphor. Engel knows we cannot
mute our hearts. Without love we cannot return home. Let us hope
love does not arrive blindfolded. Engel reminds us that love is water
and what we have always thirst for is peace. We need the water to stop
the burning, to end the fire that consumes us each day. We need to
inhale hope not smoke. It is Kathy Engel who tells us it's not too
late to make music and to dance by the sea. It is not too late
to forgive ourselves.

–E. Ethelbert Miller, Writer and Literary Activist
2023 Grammy Nominated Finalist in the category of Spoken Word and Poetry

I

From now

Spring, 2020 (quarantine)

you will never forget the miles across the sea from   say

Delhi to New York   are nothing   really   you want

to learn the language of a four-legged   winged   finned   river

birch & sunset maple   you watch piping plovers still

gather & lift in unison as if they are the ghosts

growing

you bow down to nurses & truck drivers   farmers,

scientists, teachers & single mothers guiding children

while working in one room homes & those

without one room   to the clearing sea   chance of day   gift of lung

you know contamination is cells within you

ticking

you dare to speak   dare not to   or walk

to nowhere & somewhere   rest when you should

be working   you should not be working   there will

be no *you*   only the *I* who has become a *we*

flesh made of earth   skin of sky   pleading breath

water

Falling

perhaps because
I was rushing, not paying
attention, or empathy for
Yesenia who fell the day
before, perhaps because
my body knew after falling
that I'd just heard yet another story
from someone I call sister
who is a Black woman
in this America about doing big
work then getting shafted
by white women.   I've witnessed
these stories, no doubt somehow,
at a time specific or not
have been complicit even if by
not standing strong enough
speaking loud enough or not
at all, not trusting
what I deeply know.   I thought
maybe I should retire early
to open a space for a Black
woman; in universities more

Black, Brown, Indigenous,
women of color are teased
with adjunct or visiting
carrot than offered full
course meal – over a box in my
office hard & awkward, bending
my arm, yelled at two sweet
students who came running in:
I'm fine! I'm fine! (get out!)
Maybe I fell
because no part of me knows
what theory, artmaking
or structure will adequately address
the unforgivable.
So
I fall. & get up. Not
alone —
with the stories
my body plants,
carries
& hoards

The Gift

I opened my body

like an envelope

collarbone

to pelvic tip

found a thousand

masks   different

sizes   faded

wrinkled

made of gauze

ribbon

one was gold

I reached in

disentangled

them one by one

from kidney liver rib

cage   one tucked

inside my womb

as home   turned

into a red tulip

when it hit the air

a few grew wings

& flew

I laid the others

on the table

where we eat

disinfected them

with toxic spray

I'd never used

before   I'd planned

to give them to you

to show I care

but each time I reached

with gloved hands

to pick one up

it grew fangs

Breaching & Sounding

we who built a life together
watch in the distant green sea
just after dawn as the world
pauses & still careens
into human made oblivion
sparkle   a spout rising
into cobalt

the whale's
ancient inky body awes
me to quiet as J. narrates
run-on & staccato as a 5-
year-old with a worm
we grab elbow   thigh
pinching   to be sure

some of *us who did* not die
crawl into morning
crabs holding onto what hasn't
disappeared
in the bludgeoning night
& scrawl into the world
I've been here   I loved

Unmarked Graves of Indigenous Children, 2021

"751 Unmarked Graves Discovered Near Former Indigenous School in Canada… Experts estimate 4,000 to 10,000 children may have died at the schools, often from a combination of poor living conditions and disease…"
–Smithsonian Magazine, June 28, 2021

[Since 2021, more bodies have been found on sites of additional former boarding schools, including in the United States. Some children ran away and froze to death.]

1.

I will not write a poem

    over the graves of children

        the invisible calligraphy of their lives

small bonesong wrested into no zone

    no lyric from soil composted

        with veins & seeds

        gouging grammar kidnaps first truth

            of a child from their body

                no metaphor lifts the mother's ache

        blasphemy of naming, sorting, discarding

            the young

                for slaughter

some species kill

      to survive

         mine   for what

    never again say: be *more human,*

       humane

         unless you mean brutal

2.

   to honor the children

     I will study the snail in its trail,

       democracy of birds in flight

   the way trees converse & I'll

     more than hug the tree, will stroke

     & hold as long as I can,

     awkward, unknowing, reverent:

mother of all mimosas growing in all directions,

    pink puffs so luscious they could gag a cynic —

     give me a language

    for the stem that loves the root

     fully; the root

     that holds the stem

     with all that is

      sacred

Haiku without writing the word *(pandemic)*

the short night becomes
long, moon holds strong, stars tease my
sky, this body shakes

I Should Have Married You Sooner

dear reader, I should have offered you a light-filled room
with blue walls & paintings by loved ones & strangers

left a flowy red silk dress on the bed
deer antler & turkey feather on the oak desk

a corner in the garden for planting favorite herbs
swarm of bees, netted head covering & glass jar

your own blank label for marking sting, sweet,
extinction & survival, compost bucket & shovel,

ceramic bowl J. made filled with blue-green
ocean water for blessing, a handwritten

numbered guide to resisting enemies of memory
which means enemies of love & its messes

a copy of Hikmet's *Things I Didn't Know I Loved*
& the beginning of a next line to use as you choose

Do-over

Start with softness of horse muzzle without the violence of harness
                    stay there in clover
The parents agree on the value of such close animal breath
The girl gallops with abandon, no rupture
The parents make a nice divorce, converse with regard
The big brother finds a place in his body where he can live
Somehow the family learns ok is enough
Somehow the family learns love is not a contest
The family learns vulnerable can melt in the mouth like butter even when sour
Stepdad unbreaks his back & siphons the vodka back out of the coke can
Mom finds there's no perfect, loves herself more than a measuring cup
Before & after death Dad holds failure like a peony, petals open then falling
My beloved & I believe each wants the best for the other
Our daughters think the world of themselves
Let's say we all know how to forgive ourselves

Let's say we all know how to forgive ourselves
Our daughters think the world of themselves
My beloved & I believe each wants the best for the other
Before & after death Dad holds failure like a peony, petals open then falling
Mom finds there's no perfect, loves herself more than a measuring cup
Stepdad unbreaks his back & siphons the vodka back out of the coke can
The family learns vulnerable can melt in the mouth like butter even when sour

Somehow the family learns love is not a contest

Somehow the family learns ok is enough

The big brother finds a place in his body where he can live

The parents make a nice divorce, converse with regard

The girl gallops with abandon, no rupture

The parents agree on the value of such close animal breath

Start with softness of horse muzzle without the violence of harness

        stay there in clover

II

August letter to a poet

This gorgeous country loves to make a summer
orphan or take a parent's child. The tree will soon
articulate its loss, first flush, then naked limbs.
Geese announce their discipline. What can I
discover from their V-shaped flight?
My dear brother, you claim faith in poems
to get us through attempted murder
of the soul. Let's hold June's words
the willingness to listen and to say all that we know
until they bloom to flame, then turn them
into water, spray everything we find with
or without the chance to grow. Who's to say
the likelihood? Let's train each muscle's syllabus
of love no matter the attempts to rip it raw.
The bridge under my bare feet, time-filled
body & yours, is rickety, yet someone
drew its design, measured, cut & nailed.
Now with spit, paste, memory, hammer,
grit & what's still not known, we'll mend
each part & keep walking

February, 2021: 11 months pandemic

1.
I plan to barter
with nothing to offer

only stray syllables
so I hide in my lab

punctuate   erase   test
serum after serum

green tea   argan
lavish away

stagnation
excavate

infestation
what's real

on my skin
in nervous system

social system
what I can't change

or might
with sharper optic

nerve   with you
so I coconut   I oil

gloss   cheeks
thighs   mouth

paint deep red
over fissure

draw black
kohl line

through border
pull on tiger

leggings   snake
sweater   leopard

rimmed glasses
all my animal

all my masks

2.
cold morning, done masking
cement heavy, beyond number

who is under, or no longer
who beyond sight or touch

endless eyes die alone
invaded   by all the things

we know & don't
what grammar can I

tack on with meaning
       – these eyes in this one

body have seen land
mine   lips   shell fragments

on ground like puzzle
pieces   tiny limbs shattered

heard words milked
from shrapnel breasts

kidnapped   & each
time I've returned

from war to the walls
of home   now I'm

terrified to register
the hollows of today

For that hour

it's the icefloes I can't stop
thinking about, cascade of endless
blue, lonely cold

& faces of grieving mothers
I'll always see, year after
year, country after country –

tonight I pray especially
for India, Gaza, Colombia & here
& here   & yet to name may be

to exclude – the list doesn't end
always fragmented
like memory, broken shell

& we are more than the names
of places, more than lists –
ache of separation knows

no border   no time zone;
Vandana's seeds promise
for every loss a planting –

today, against the backdrop

of nonstop war, I sat on the floor

with Carolina & Paola, sisters –

my tia arms rocked their babies

born just weeks apart

to sweet sleep – tiny frog legs,

bellies softening, faces up toward

whatever's there & for that hour

listening to the beautiful mamas

I knew as children, me telling

early stories of my babies,

their sister friends, Ella & Jaja,

time evaporated,

everything once again

possible, each sudden twitch,

skin smelling so new

–May, 2021

Let me promise something real

[The] small pinecones
dangle from tall trees

[they] look like fingers

I attempt re   vision
delete [the] article

to strengthen [the] noun
for [the] sake of concision

to be
less

conspicuous

I'm wrong!

[the] extraction is meaningless
cost me nothing & I know

if I don't write down /
leave [a] hem of here ness

oil stain   smudge   not just
cones but sap splurging out

of pine's trunk
I'll leave an even worse

mess   oh
grammar of longing

& be longing   unstitch
this throat   lend me

a language of sky

Now listen

*On the occasion of the rescinding of Angela Davis's Fred Shuttleworth
Award by The Birmingham Civil Rights Institute*

I am a white
Jewish American
woman
I've seen uprooted
syllables
of Palestinian
verse knotted
in a fenced village
guns planted
like trees
I've heard
Black American
mothers
locked up
for being
themselves
recite
their children's
names as anthem
Dear Birmingham
you can't rescind
a daughter:
Angela
messenger
of the gods
you can't un
light
a torch

What could the title possibly be

He kissed his wife & kids
maybe he wished them a good
day in Spanish, maybe in some
form of North American
English, maybe some other way,
maybe he said *see you tonight,*
maybe stopped at the door
turned around: *I love you,*
got into the car, went to the first
of two jobs. He'd been working
at the restaurant for ten years.
He was *loved.* He was
diligent. A *model citizen.*
Some good voters with money
in the bank wearing white
headlights I mean skin were
stunned this could happen so
close to home. So close to
the expensive food he served
them. The card, green as the
lawns, was in the mail. Some
authority said. Another said
that doesn't matter.

The sheriff at the local jail said
sure we'll keep him. The local
democrats said *it's ok, it's only*
ICE, meaning not US. The
weekly printed he had an old
DWI. When they took him
they forgot to tell him
anything. When they took him
across states & borders
with no access to counsel
they neglected to remember
he was a man with a family
& a place he now called home,
holding more than one job. They
did remember he was brown
spoke a language many didn't
understand, from a hot country
green as the missing card.
They did remember
it didn't matter. When they
took Luis they were just
doing their job.

Where I Live

We returned to the tangle of place called home in 1994 — me, my husband, and our young daughters. I was afraid of it, terrified of myself in it, loved it the way you love food you think you're not supposed to eat and fear will make you sick.

This is where when I was a child Claribel the angry Angus cow taught me caution.

This is where Trill, the Welsh pony, reared up each time I attempted to slip my leg over her back, my stepfather, the farmer, and his brother trying to hold her down.

This is where my mother and her friends showed me how to start something (a school) in your community, at the kitchen table.

This is where the vast salt ocean and rough wind soothed my agitated mind; I learned that in the physical world one could locate a sense of belonging and mystery.

This is where I got the train from the spit of a stop in Bridgehampton back to my father's life — the city and its grit, activism, my Jewishness, art. This is where I was the only Jewish kid in John Marshall Elementary School. This is where I learned to hide my fear.

This is where I couldn't/can't hide. Because it's where I live. The fields, sea, the spectacular beauty, the farmers and what they grow, my family, and the bald glare of contradiction and old plantation segregation.

This is where the landscape of race rode up on me, closed like a barn door locking in the rat of injustice.

This is where I saw how people live in daily acceptance of inequity and don't name it.

This is where I sometimes joined on the harvester after school.

This is where I sometimes rode in the pickup truck with my stepfather to take Geraldine, who was Black and from the South and up here to pick potatoes, back to her shack a few miles from our so comfortable barn-turned-home near the beach.

This is where Geraldine and the others working the harvester welcomed me, showed me how to pick out the bad ones, toss them off to the side — dirt on my hands, brush of wind, red crank of the tractor, the stories, her pipe and deep voice.

And this is where something felt so wrong when I saw where she lived — the tattoo of two worlds divided by train tracks. This is where those who lived on the Turnpike didn't make that decision, didn't say: We want to live here in shacks while you have your bigger homes across the tracks and we take care of your kids, clean your messes, and pick your potatoes.

This is where in fourth grade I witnessed a young Black girl slammed against a cement wall by a white gym teacher, couldn't shake my inability to intervene, a rock of guilty silence lodged in my abdomen, prodding me like a knife.

This is where as a young woman I returned after travel to war zones. This is where the summer of '82 I was called an ignorant self-hating commie in the letters section of my local newspaper after writing that American Jews (me) should protest Israel's invasion of Lebanon.

This is where when we decided to come home, a number of progressive white friends said: You're moving there? Why? And most of my friends of color said: That's wonderful. Can't wait to visit. And did.

This is where whenever someone visited for the first time I was afraid she or he would judge me, find out my secret.

This is where I returned. To live inside contradiction.

This is where once a week as I write my poems or take a run, a woman from Central America cleans my house.

This is where more than one Black woman friend traveling on the bus from the city to visit us was asked by a white woman sitting next to her: Oh, are you going to work?

This is where, in our backyard, under the mimosa tree, we laugh in that uneasy way when the friends report the story over pasta and poems, as I step back from the squirm of my whiteness.

This is where when our younger daughter was in high school some of her white classmates threatened her Latinx and African-American classmates, made swastikas and emblems of white supremacy, so a group of us, parents and teachers, formed a committee. This is where the Black former teachers and administrators told about their daily pain working at the school. We didn't use the phrase white supremacy. This is where the committee soon stopped talking about race and focused on drugs and alcohol. This is where I learned that drugs and alcohol don't discriminate, even though law enforcement does. This is where I knew that project was urgent, tapping into my own scab and flood of denial. At the same time this is where discussion of race was once again erased.

This is where our older daughter and her friends were told to return after volunteering in New Orleans post-Katrina. The leaders of the unlearning racism workshop led by the People's Institute for Survival and Beyond instructed the group to go home and find the Katrina in their own communities.

Here the hurricane lives underneath the belly of the good life and enlightened conversation.

This is where the storm lives, where I live, in my body and the body of the split. In the ZIP code 11962. Under our floorboards. On Shinnecock land.

Where many who speak the language of Lorca are called alien while digging up weeds in other people's gardens and mopping other people's floors, often living crammed in motel rooms and also running businesses or making art.

Here not all residents go to Pilates classes and the ocean on weekends.

This is where it's hard to find a hair salon that does Black hair. Unless you know who's opened up shop in her living room.

This is where my paragraphs break down because I'm afraid of what I'm writing. It will never be right. I will never be right in it.

This is where I returned after standing on the bridge in Selma to mark the 50th anniversary of the bloody march. And couldn't move for a moment. And couldn't write about it. Couldn't find an adequacy of language in my throat.

This is where as in so many wheres I often hear white people asking the one or two persons of color in the room to be the expert, the wizard of addressing race, the flag carrier, burdened by teaching.

Where the mirror is confused.

This is where I get calls and emails from people who identify as white asking if I could recommend a person of color for their activity. I believe they are driven toward inclusivity and change. At the same time I want to suggest they ask themselves what prevents them from knowing Black or brown people where they live. Will white people fight white supremacy living in isolation, when the reality can be turned on and off like a TV show?

This is where I fear alienating friends and neighbors.

This is where this summer, 2016, I march with my daughters, mother, and husband in support of Black Lives Matter in our villages, following new local leadership. Where in our home we make signs as we've always done. This time: Black Lives Matter/White Silence Kills. And our older daughter's boyfriend, who is white, joins, for whom this is a first. This is where I know again that the young leaders of Black Lives Matter are doing my job for me.

This is where I sit with my coffee after a dunk in the magnificent Atlantic, watching the strolling turkey family, small chicks, and a lone big-antlered buck on our nearly two acres. I hear my best friend's voice. A brilliant and acclaimed writer, a Black woman, and our daughters' godmother, she recently said to me: "I want to wake up one day and hear that people who identify as white are calling the demonstrations so we who are being killed can stay home for a change." Her voice vibrates in my chest.

This is where one of the people who has bravely stepped up where we live was a friend of our older daughter from high school days. A young Black man, it turns out he is the son of a man who worked for and alongside my white stepfather, the farmer.

This is where I live. I am steeped in the story. I seek an ethical, lyrical language and the courage to do the next right thing. To end the systemic, structural denial and brutality that is white supremacy and is killing us, and my participation in it. So we can all live well where we live.

This is where I live, in this gift of a place, in this particular America, where in mid-August on a Monday evening I go to enjoy Escola de Samba BOOM, the band my husband and a number of friends play with, on the beach, under a nearly full moon, kids of all sizes and colors dancing in the ocean and on the sand, the sound of multiple languages infusing the air, piping plovers still alive. A truly community formation, when I look around, inhale, it smells like hope, it tastes like joy, the sweat and beam emanating from a group of people who resemble the world. For an hour. Making music, in music. By the sea.

–2016

What's Another Word for Genocide?

> *Whole families, my neighbors are killed. We left our house on*
> *Thursday. Two hours ago, I just went back home to get some food*
> *and clothes. And just a few minutes ago, they bombed my neighbors.*
> *They are dead. We are dead.*

–Mosab Abu-Toha, Gaza, October 14, 2023

Dear Mosab   are you there
can you hear the voices reading
your poems into terrified air
here   there   we saw it coming

did we   this   &   today I stood at
the shore   recalled a summer photo
you at the sea in Gaza   said you
wanted all to know her beauty

in April you told my students
a poem starts anywhere   one
small drop of water traveling   that's
what I remember you saying

softly to their thirst   now
no water   I hoard your words
repeat them as prayer   wear them
as shawl   close to the skin   how

do I dare   from here   this   but
my government can stop it
instead uses taxes I pay
from *teaching* to fire white

phosphorous   steal the sky
from dream   pummeling stones
that built homes like arrows
into flesh   you write &

write   the body-filled death
bed of fire   split open
when will you get food again
who is sleeping at all   even

the questions violate
earth   some things not to be
imagined   are red juicy strawberries still
rising up out of the thrashed earth

where I am the ocean glimmers
greenblue   deceptively calm   where
is *where*   we saw this   coming
but   no   not   couldn't   I

call up my ghosts who fled
a pogrom   even the blue &
black birds this morning
screech & flap   CEASEFIRE

CEASEFIRE   the only word
they are mourning   they are
telling   no borders in the air
who in the world could believe

who could look away   the waves
between us wail   shudder
tides ache dragging fragments
of memory in shattered boats

stripped pages   no rudder   no sail
where is *there*   your poems walk
me from place to place   I search
usefulness in a mirror of horror

this is not a new story   worse
no words I can carve   *We are dead*
you write   what's another word
for genocide   I'm afraid to ask

about the library   did books check
themselves out first   another word
for complicity   I send my love
the only way I know how

does it arrive blind
folded   shredded   between
missiles or become one   arrive
at all   love is an action   is

it water   if I could turn
myself into a current rushing
to stop the burn that is home
that was   quench a child's throat

if I could surge such blessings
sea to sea   be water
channeling to another air   I
frantically try to make a better

poem for you   as though it
could   can you feel mouths
everywhere ushering your words
each small drop of [holy] water

an ocean

– For Mosab and the people of Gaza, October 19, 2023

Seahorse tanka

he carries the eggs

body twice-curved, salted, she/

he dips water, mates

for life, four to six years to

court, tails entwine   to mourn, wait

Ownership   a haibun

I want to stay in the miracle of small yellow & purple flowers popping up around the mimosa which some call a weed, whose pink puffs waft out of their pods each summer without fail; I mean leaning over on all fours to look & inhale for longer than I can ever sit reading a book or writing; I mean wallow in the delicate spreading beauty that is absolutely perfect while not so many yards away the ground is persistently slaughtered, *owners* dosing, jabbing, cutting the loveliness out of the land their ancestors stole; I guess making sure to be clear that it's theirs to hatchet & maul & I have to ask myself how does our planting fit into this picture?

no one can own earth
or water – & I too am
incriminated

Only (Gaza again)

read a verse by a
Palestinian each day
make words into home

   * * *

eyelid, silk, letters
collected – nothing – can yes
find a place named home

   * * *

standing with a sign
again, against the kill, &
for? simply your home

   * * *

what can a few words
falling with summer rain tell
the drenched soul's torn home

   * * *

only stones remain
drones hover & whir lighting
the olive night, home

* * *

this young one gone, a
piece of thick brown hair still stuck,
old eyes – what is home

* * *

truce at summer's end,
here mimosa sheds pink puffs,
body parts, a home

* * *

no place to bury
the dead I read, newsprint, blurred
traces beckon home

* * *

never again will
I mute my heart, I say your
name, Gaza, old home

–2014

Post script: 65

I try to learn serenity
with peeling pink river birch,
wave's white curl & snarl,
knowing arrival means death
so instead I extend ritual
to point ridiculous

ask permission of spotted
sycamore, namesake of
my mother's childhood road,
to touch its layered bark,
tree my grandfather tried
to teach me that only
now I recognize

I spit a waterfall of out-
loud thank yous, talk with
my dead, add to the list
as it grows – fear of
neglecting any ghost, fear
the atlas of forgiveness
might edit to deletion, starve –

at the shore again, thick
black coffee in favorite mugs,
tremor of waking fades
as we inhale sea & J.
tells me that it's possible
to stand inside a cloud
& we are doing it right now

June letter to bff

because June introduced us
   the 12th day of June
thirty-seven years ago
from a soapbox you spoke poems
on a street corner at the center
of a universe, a million humans
snake dancing the streets, drums,
puppets, shadows cloaking monks
from Nagasaki

because the tearing of separation
a map we were blasting open
& sewing   but the people
of peace wouldn't say
Palestine   remember that?
   because I'm grasping
for meaning & last week
also in June your goddaughter read
your *Enchanted Hair Tale*

for a hungry congregation –
the spirited boy,
his festival of dreadlocks

　　where is he now, with what mouth
can we hold his name today
black as love
Sudan　Sudan
where have you gone,
are you a man

walked out of the story,
escaped the sentence
of night, namesake,
what light can humans make
of our redundant bodies,
what interruption,
who can we keep
alive

– June, 2019

To those with whom I learn

when I can walk into a room ready to listen, tentacles
alive & fuzzy as the caterpillar crossing the road
after rain, endangered as the slow turtle, its shell

a scripture, thirsty as sun parched gingko in August;
when I can sit or stand with you not poised to show
what I know or pressed into the flex of legibility

that can't read or translate my body or yours;
when I can open my arms that are my home
& inhale – what you can teach me,

what can be made together in the multiverse;
then perhaps I can trust I don't need to call myself
anything more than becoming

Horse

oh you horse
your shiny mahogany coat
& the chestnut on the inside
of your leg, vestigial toe
of Eohippus, a fingerprint,
night eye looking out,
cave wall drawing, still

Message to self on 63rd birthday

Tell your hurried breath you'll give up the race to be admired.

Let the dazzling bones of those you've lost light the way.

Listen to their haunting rasp & rhyme. Soon

you'll be dust too, joining an out-of-tune chorus. Wild

time to open the body's space like a sail. Remember

the language you yearn to become. Be dangerously loyal to that.

You might lose your job when you wear those riotous syllables,

naked sonnet slicing the night or flag stitched from the slogan

rich t-shirts you flaunt. You might fail those you love.

Again. So easily you don't notice as it happens. You might

fail your own desire to be brave. So what. Luscious salt waves

keep taking you back. Now, tell your beloveds, all those animal lives:

what whets your appetite for dawn's curved entrance is everyday

thorn, a field of questions, the radiant halt & start of nearness

–2018

When the body

abandons the spirit with whom it partnered,
even when sparring, even when unaligned, or dis
located, even as sight scorches the lie of time,
or even when the severing is slow; what, beloved
unfaithful evening, what if the mind still stirs
a thousand wild ways, racketing against the softening
of cartilage; what then?

& Earth said

our heart is broken
she/they said   but we will carry
on   whether you will
is unclear   water knows   air
does   be volta   ~~like~~ with us

I'm not a day you
know   I'm who you are & what
you're of   who you need
I'm us   I'm we   what you see
this turning churning is real

–April 22, 2021

I return

to the horses
       like a divining rod pulled to water
             under morning gibbous   lick pink frosted dawn
      as they do the salt block

      mittened hand   winter bare
           feet   left out of driveway
       big windowed home
          land stays stolen (swollen?)

past tree mouth   root twist   wind-wrenched trunk
      the weight of it   I lean into & sniff dappled
          sycamore   lean on cedar fence separating
     the horses & me   call to the bay

     the grey   tails long & full   no *human* near
       to interpret or squelch
        my most visceral   un
        conditional

        I call
       loud to the horses
       how you doing today?
one nods   head up   shakes   snorts   what

do they know of pre-dawn terror
    grief   killer ego   what do they
        know of greed   full eyes radaring out
velvety muzzles   tentacle whiskers

      hooves slice a narrow path in the grass
        they know what they know   in their ways
    of knowing   I'm impatient
          leaning & calling

It would be water

how it comes from the sky because I am dry   because
I am thirsty   reaching down for roots I can feel
& up for dream & because I need the wet the release
of flood   but not too much   that would have been the daily
April poem then I snuck into a little place for pasta   talked
myself into believing I deserved a treat   thinking I was
anonymous   & there was Meena's husband David with friends
eating & laughing   we greeted awkwardly   I stayed at my
corner table   red wine & rigatoni   all I could think about was
Meena's thick shiny nearly black hair   how I didn't manage
to visit her that last year of illness although I said I would
she sent me poem & photo   told about losing her hair
I said it looks beautiful short   that I was thinking of cutting
mine   don't do it she said   don't cut your hair then she
was gone   her photo in my office so anyone who enters
will know   her poems moving around like waves   tulip
stems   high pitched elegant voice articulating
how the world begins & ends   how verse continues

When I was a crow

I saw things
more clearly, from the ground
or on top of a pole
beak nod, head turn,
my dark pinpoint eyes
surveyed miles, drawn to death's flesh

when I was coffee I realized
my pungent power, also the
back & hand pain suffered
by those who picked me as oily
bean — I thought there must be
another way to drink my addictive gift

when I was gull I kept
my secrets close, tucked under
salty wing, greyish, never far
from tide's endless turning
I knew whale, shark, finfish,
defined my own beauty, my churning

when I was new green spear
of grass I reached up fast as
I could, knowing the air is
ours, hoping to evade
the blade, motors whose handlers
regard me as something to control

when I was a horse
I was myself, snorted, side
stepped, lay in the field
with my moody girl, until
she thought she must outgrow
our warm breathy interspecies

now that I am of the gaggle
I know where to fly, trust
the geometry of collective
travel, distinct resonant signal,
when cold comes early we discuss
imminence   departure/return/again

Sea life landay

mother & pup sea otter sleep hand
in hand to not lose each other in the night   mama

This beauty could lull me to forgetfulness

in the open quiet staring toward fawn's
big eyes staring back   stopped still

I ask myself   can I be question

surge of plant dust   yellow succulence
a zillion casts of green   who is

my enemy within   what is our tango?

What if

I say good morning to my neighbor, the grazing grey dappled horse
in the field, who looks up, shakes his head, flicks his tail & one

by one I take the fence's wooden rails out of their post holes,
lay them on the ground *free to go* I say, tickled with myself,

no more girth around belly, no more bit pulling the sides of mouth,
no more heels digging into ribs, no more cooing or commanding voice,

then remember this beauty trotting & snorting was castrated by a hu-
man, fed by, spurred & reined in by   what will he do now roaming through

paved roads, metal, pesticides & roaring trucks   will he find food,
lay down safely, stand, gallop – can he find his herd

Garden

my beloved drops shoes
anywhere the way a bunny
drops shit, leaves doors
open, bath running, burner on
   but when it comes to worms,
seeds, dirt   he's on it!
   tall outlaw mullein bursts
a yellow crown, garlic scape
bends & swans its white-
tipped kisses – even dry
forsythia sticks like divining
rods poked in the ground bloom
deep green; slate slabs might
grow words –
   no dead here –
this sandy soil defies its
fallow past   turkey family
& deer party til dawn, gingko
leaves twirl, red-winged black
bird signals as J. stoops over,
breath combing the ground
he loves, hands turning

Dear inheritors

dear bookend, dear crow in tree, dear stutter,
rupture, rapture, hole in the eye

of remembering

dear fingernail scratching boat railing,
childhood ending, dear buffalo, whale, human

& snail

dear worn out adjective, nameless year
& month   dear

welcome:

*   *   *

dear inheritors:
today will not be called day
i will not be called i

death has no reason
stars can't be captured –
if it's a flag

let's strip the borders
& call it
moving through together

an imaginary loom awaits me
with rough hands I weave
silk & burlap strands

stalk an unmade
heaven
right here

* * *

I did count on each batch
of mistakes
to feed

a multitude of small
victories
pink light

* * *

it turns out translation *is*
every thing after all &
nearly impossible

my dreamy map
to an imaginary *we*
flails, grasps & gasps

*   *   *

what can I offer you now?
this
just this –

these ears re-
born each dawn
out of sleep's

restless tunnel
these still strong arms
even from afar

these eyes learning
such beauty in dead things
surprise in the living

Notes:

"Falling": Yesenia is poet Yesenia Montilla

"Breaching & sounding": "some of us *who did not die*" borrowed from June Jordan's book entitled *Some of Us Did Not Die*)

"I should have married you sooner": the title and beginning of first line are borrowed from a line from Major Jackson's poem "Let Me Begin Again": *Dear reader, I should have married you sooner…*

"Do-over": is after Warsan Shire's poem "Backwards," borrowing specifically from her line *…Step-Dad spits liquor back into glass…*

"August letter to a poet": is for poet E. Ethelbert Miller in response to an email he sent to friends in 2017 regarding the state of the world and what poems offer. The quote from *June* is June Jordan, from her "Letter To My Friend," *Civil Wars.*

"Let me promise something real": *Wrong!* is borrowed from my great nephew Henry who jubilantly exclaimed *I'm wrong!* when learning he had mistaken one person for another at daycare pick-up time.

"Now listen": is for Angela Davis, with appreciation to Cornelius Eady for the repeating line *I am a Black American poet* in his poem "Gratitude." The name Angela means *messenger of the Gods.*

"For that hour": the reference to icefloes is connected to a collaboration with visual artist Ellen Driscoll whose work includes images of glaciers and other disappearing things. Vandana is the writer, activist leader, and scholar Vandana Shiva.

"Only (Gaza again)": *…only stones remain…*drawn from *Al Jazeera*, July, 2014.

"It would be water": is in memory of poet Meena Alexander.

"To those with whom I learn": is for my students, past & present, with whom I learn.

"June letter to bff": (1.) My bff is poet/writer Alexis De Veaux. June (introduced us…) refers to June Jordan. (2.) "The Enchanted Hair Tale" is an award-winning children's book by Alexis De Veaux, in which the main character is named Sudan. (3.) June 12, 1982, was the great march and rally in NYC for Disarmament & Human Needs for which I was the Lead Cultural Coordinator. (4.) *Your goddaughter* refers to my daughter Ella. (5.) Reference to Sudan: The Khartoum massacre occurred on 3 June 2019, when the armed forces of the Sudanese Transitional Military Council used heavy gunfire and teargas to disperse a sit-in by protestors in Khartoum, killing more than 100 people. (6.) June 12, 1982 is the birth date of writer Alexis Pauline Gumbs.

"Horse": is after "Giraffe" by Talia, PS 276, 2nd grade, NYC, A *Poem for your pocket* project (year unknown) with Poet's House. This poem is for my daughter Jaja and her students.

"Dear Inheritors": (1.) I realized long after writing the line and the poem that my daughter Ella also uses the line "What can I offer you now…" in one of her poems, entitled "somber days I write for the collards." (2.) The line and ½ *Dear fingernail scratching boat railing, // childhood ending* was in some way inspired by a line by the writer Fivos Botsis's poem "Dare to Sing."

Acknowledgements:

I gratefully acknowledge the following journals, anthologies, newspapers and online sites for publishing some of the writings in this collection, at times in an earlier version:

Borderlines, Poems of Migration (anthology): "What could the title possibly be"

Platform Review: "From now," "June letter to bff," "Haiku without saying the word (pandemic)," "Message to self on 63rd birthday"

Portside: "Falling" and "Now listen"

The East Hampton Star and *The Boggs Center to Nurture Community Leadership* newsletter: "Where I Live"

About Place: "August letter to a poet"

NOW 2, Hobart Women Writers Festival Online Journal: "The gift"

At the Crossroads, an anthology of One Breath Rising (forthcoming):
     "What if," "And earth said," "Unmarked Graves of Indigenous Children"

Academy of American Poets Poem A Day: "It would be water"

The Mom Egg: "For that hour," "Postscript: 65," "When the body"

Vox Populi: "What's Another Word for Genocide"

"This beauty could lull me to forgetfulness," "Seahorse tanka," "Horse," "When the body," and "Dear Inheritors" are part of "Eyechart," a collaboration with the visual artist Ellen Driscoll, appearing in multiple forms and iterations.

Photo by author

Thank You

So many, here and no longer, make it possible for me to write, to dare to share what I write, to even exist. I'll never be able to name you all. I hope you know. I hope I've expressed gratitude and also shown you the love you deserve. I know I don't always. I keep trying. Thank you for your patience

Thank you for supporting the process of this work in multiple ways and inspiring me with your work:

Judith Vollmer for the intensely generous attention to and faith in this book over months and months

Roberto Carlos Garcia for the caring, painstaking labor of love that Get Fresh Books is, for hanging in with my quirks and challenges, for the risk and gift of bringing poetry books into the world

The whole Get Fresh Books team

Darlene Charneco for the generosity of your stunning art, your visionary, loving spirit

E. Ethelbert Miller for faithful support year after year, your big literary activism

Alexis Pauline Gumbs for radiant love work in the world, and for the care and thought in reading this book and offering your words

Kimberly Blaeser for the trust, generous reading, writing, for the radiance of your work & sisterness

Kindall Gant for generously, thoughtfully, helping this book find its places in the world

Alexis De Veaux for showing me how writing lives, as border crosser, as self definer, as expansive, daring, ever growing, as there-for-one-another in all the ways

Thank you each …

Sonia Sanchez, Yesenia Montilla, Nathalie Handal, Aracelis Girmay, Elisa Biagini, Mihaela Moscaliuc, Michael Waters, Ross Gay, Rev. Kimberly Quinn Johnson, Patrick Rosal, Ellyn Toscano, Vangile Gantsho, Luis Rincon Alba, Refilwe Nkomo, Maia Marie, Sangodare Wallace, Sokare Ekine, Moses Family, Pato Hebert, Alison Meyers, Naimah L. Holmes, Tiye Giraud, Leslie Cagan, Phyllis Bennis, Allyson Pimentale, Pedro Noguera, Cheryl Boyce Taylor, Gale Jackson, Sandra Garcia Betancourt, Melissa Tuckey, Adonis Volanakis, Ella Shohat, Gwendolen Hardwick, Naomi Shihab Nye, Steven Fullwood, Mosab Abu Toha, Alia Al-Sabi, Joanna Evans, Narkita Wiley, Nick Bazzano (for saving the book)… so many more…

Lalela Collaborative Poetics sisters

Elma's Heart Circle sister poets

NYU Tisch Department of Art & Public Policy

Hobart Festival of Women Writers

Enclave Habitat

Ellen Driscoll for your amazing art, for EYECHART
Philippe Cheng, once again for your generous eye

thank you NYU Faculty for Justice in Palestine, East End for Ceasefire, Middle East Children's Alliance, MADRE, Jewish Voice for Peace …

to all those with whom I learn; we are each other's students… you know who you are…thank you deeply

and those no longer here, still teaching me, thank you, ongoing

especially, now, Herman J. Engel, who stood for/with what he believed. And stood with me as I did, even when it was hard

Tim Engel, Kamal Boullata, June Jordan, Valerie J. Maynard, Safiya Henderson Holmes, Ingrid Washinawatok, Grace Paley, Grace Lee Boggs and …

Family, all, sisters, again, always – steadfast, funny, wise, loving – partners, siblings in-love, nephews, nieces, kids… special welcome to the new ones! Thank you Henry for naming and participating in our *Trail of Poems!* That gave me such joy

Mom, continuing to amaze in your curiosity, care, gutsy vibrancy and steadfast showing up

Jon, beloved, hands in the earth, building life together, through it all, we continue to grow & love and live

Ella and Jaja, every day, my lights, you show me what integrity is, what unconditional love is, what humility is, what hard work is, remind me to laugh at myself, inspire me

And to you who take the time to read these poems. Thank you. I hope they offer something of use.

Photo by Philippe Cheng

Kathy Engel

Co-started, imagined, coordinated/curated a bunch of projects with many others, including the cultural component of June 12, 1982 March for Disarmament and Human Rights, *talking nicaragua*, Moving Towards Home, MADRE (which she directed for five years), Riptide Communications, *Stand With Sisters for Economic Dignity*, *Who I Will Be*, Poets for Ayiti, Hayground School, KickAss Artists, Lyrical Democracies, East End for Peace, East End Women in Black… co-edited with Kamal Boullata, *We Begin Here: Poems for Palestine and Lebanon*. Other books include *Ruth's Skirts*, *The Lost Brother Alphabet*.

She teaches, meaning co-learns, at New York University in the Department of Art & Public Policy.

The rest is in the poems, she hopes. And the in betweens.